Essays

Essays
Francis Bacon

MINT EDITIONS

Essays was first published in 1597.

This edition published by Mint Editions 2021.

ISBN 9781513267777 | E-ISBN 9781513272771

Published by Mint Editions®

minteditionbooks.com

Publishing Director: Jennifer Newens
Design & Production: Rachel Lopez Metzger
Typesetting: Westchester Publishing Services

Contents

Chapter 1

OF TRUTH

What is truth? said jesting Pilate; and would not stay for an answer. Certainly, there be that delight in giddiness; and count it a bondage to fix a belief; affecting freewill in thinking as well as in acting. And though the sects of philosophers of that kind be gone, yet there remain certain discoursing wits which are of the same veins, though there be not so much blood in them as was in those of the ancients. But it is not only the difficulty and labor which men take in finding out of truth: nor again, that, when it is found, it imposeth upon men's thoughts, that doth bring lies in favor; but a natural though corrupt love of the lie itself. One of the later schools of the Grecians examineth the matter, and is at a stand to think what should be in it that men should love lies; where neither they make for pleasure, as with poets; nor for advantage, as with the merchant, but for the lie's sake. But I cannot tell; this same truth is a naked and open daylight, that doth not show the masks, and mummeries, and triumphs of the world, half so stately and daintily as candle-lights. Truth may perhaps come to the price of a pearl, that showeth best by day, but it will not rise to the price of a diamond or carbuncle, that showeth best in varied lights. A mixture of a lie doth ever add pleasure. Doth any man doubt, that if there were taken out of men's minds vain opinions, flattering hopes, false valuations, imaginations as one would, and the like, but it would leave the minds of a number of men poor shrunken things, full of melancholy and indisposition, and unpleasing to themselves? One of the fathers, in great severity, called poesy "vinum dæmonum," because it filleth the imagination, and yet it is but with the shadow of a lie. But it is not the lie that passeth through the mind, but the lie that sinketh in, and settleth in it, that doth the hurt, such as we spake of before. But howsoever these things are thus in men's depraved judgments and affections, yet truth, which only doth judge itself, teacheth that the inquiry of truth, which is the love-making, or wooing of it, the knowledge of truth, which is the presence of it, and the belief of truth, which is the enjoying of it, is the sovereign good of human nature. The first creature of God, in the works of the days, was the light of the sense; the last was the light of reason; and his sabbath work, ever since, is the illumination of his Spirit. First, he breathed light upon the face of the matter, or chaos; then he breathed light into the face of man; and still he breatheth and inspireth light into the face of his chosen. The poet that beautified the sect, that was otherwise inferior to the rest, saith yet excellently well: "It is a pleasure to stand upon the shore, and to see ships tossed upon the sea; a pleasure to stand in the window of a castle, and to see a battle, and the adventures thereof below; but no pleasure is comparable to the standing upon the vantage-ground of truth" (a hill not to be commanded, and where the air is always clear and serene), "and to see the errors, and wanderings, and mists, and tempests, in the vale below;" so always that this prospect be with pity, and not with swelling or pride. Certainly it is heaven upon earth, to have a man's mind move in charity, rest in providence, and turn upon the poles of truth.

To pass from theological and philosophical truth to the truth of civil business; it will be acknowledged, even by those that practise it not, that clear and round dealing is the honor of man's nature, and that mixture of falsehood is like alloy in coin of gold and silver, which may make the metal work the better, but it embaseth it. For these winding and crooked courses are the goings of the serpent; which goeth basely upon the belly, and not upon the feet. There is no vice that doth so cover a man with shame, as to be found false and perfidious; and therefore Montaigne saith prettily, when he inquired the reason why the word of the lie should be such a disgrace, and such an odious charge: saith he, "If it be well weighed, to say that a man lieth, is as much as to say that he is brave towards God and a coward towards men. For a lie faces God, and shrinks from man;" surely, the wickedness of falsehood and breach of faith cannot possibly be so highly expressed, as in that it shall be the last peal to call the judgments of God upon the generations of men: it being foretold, that, when "Christ cometh," he shall not "find faith upon the earth."

Chapter 2

OF DEATH

Men fear death as children fear to go in the dark; and as that natural fear in children is increased with tales, so is the other. Certainly, the contemplation of death, as the wages of sin, and passage to another world, is holy and religious; but the fear of it, as a tribute due unto nature, is weak. Yet in religious meditations there is sometimes mixture of vanity and of superstition. You shall read in some of the friars' books of mortification, that a man should think with himself, what the pain is, if he have but his finger's end pressed or tortured; and thereby imagine what the pains of death are, when the whole body is corrupted and dissolved; when many times death passeth with less pain than the torture of a limb, for the most vital parts are not the quickest of sense. And by him that spake only as a philosopher and natural man, it was well said, "Pompa mortis magis terret, quam mors ipsa." Groans and convulsions, and a discolored face, and friends weeping, and blacks and obsequies, and the like, show death terrible. It is worthy the observing, that there is no passion in the mind of man so weak, but it mates and masters the fear of death; and therefore death is no such terrible enemy when a man hath so many attendants about him that can win the combat of him. Revenge triumphs over death; love slights it; honor aspireth to it; grief flieth to it; fear preoccupateth it; nay, we read, after Otho the emperor had slain himself, pity (which is the tenderest of affections) provoked many to die out of mere compassion to their sovereign, and as the truest sort of followers. Nay, Seneca adds niceness and satiety: "Cogita quamdiu eadem feceris; mori velle, non tantum fortis, aut miser, sed etiam fastidiosus potest." A man would die, though he were neither valiant nor miserable, only upon a weariness to do the same thing so oft over and over. It is no less worthy to observe, how little alteration in good spirits the approaches of death make: for they appear to be the same men till the last instant. Augustus Cæsar died in a compliment: "Livia, conjugii nostri memor, vive et vale." Tiberius in dissimulation, as Tacitus saith of him, "Jam Tiberium vires et corpus, non dissimulatio, deserebant:" Vespasian in a jest, sitting upon the stool, "Ut puto Deus fio;" Galba with a sentence, "Feri, si ex re sit populi Romani," holding forth his neck; Septimus Severus in dispatch, "Adeste, si quid mihi restat agendum," and the like. Certainly, the Stoics bestowed too much cost upon death, and by their great preparations made it appear more fearful. Better, saith he, "qui finem vitæ extremum inter munera ponit naturæ." It is as natural to die as to be born; and to a little infant, perhaps, the one is as painful as the other. He that dies in an earnest pursuit, is like one that is wounded in hot blood, who, for the time, scarce feels the hurt; and therefore a mind fixed and bent upon somewhat that is good, doth avert the dolors of death; but, above all, believe it, the sweetest canticle is "Nunc dimittis," when a man hath obtained worthy ends and expectations. Death hath this also, that it openeth the gate to good fame, and extinguisheth envy: "Extinctus amabitur idem."

Chapter 3

OF UNITY IN RELIGION

Religion being the chief band of human society, it is a happy thing when itself is well contained within the true band of unity. The quarrels and divisions about religion were evils unknown to the heathen. The reason was, because the religion of the heathen consisted rather in rites and ceremonies, than in any constant belief; for you may imagine what kind of faith theirs was, when the chief doctors and fathers of their church were the poets. But the true God hath this attribute, that he is a jealous God; and therefore his worship and religion will endure no mixture nor partner. We shall therefore speak a few words concerning the unity of the church; what are the fruits thereof; what the bounds; and what the means.

The fruits of unity (next unto the well-pleasing of God, which is all in all), are two; the one towards those that are without the church, the other towards those that are within. For the former, it is certain that heresies and schisms are, of all others, the greatest scandals, yea, more than corruption of manners; for as in the natural body a wound or solution of continuity is worse than a corrupt humor, so in the spiritual; so that nothing doth so much keep men out of the church, and drive men out of the church, as breach of unity; and therefore, whensoever it cometh to that pass that one saith, "Ecce in Deserto," another saith, "Ecce in penetralibus;" that is, when some men seek Christ in the conventicles of heretics, and others in an outward face of a church, that voice had need continually to sound in men's ears, "nolite exire," "go not out." The doctor of the Gentiles (the propriety of whose vocation drew him to have a special care of those without) saith: "If a heathen come in, and hear you speak with several tongues, will he not say that you are mad?" and, certainly, it is little better: when atheists and profane persons do hear of so many discordant and contrary opinions in religion, it doth avert them from the church, and maketh them "to sit down in the chair of the scorners." It is but a light thing to be vouched in so serious a matter, but yet it expresseth well the deformity. There is a master of scoffing, that, in his catalogue of books of a feigned library, sets down this title of a book, "The Morris-Dance of Heretics;" for, indeed, every sect of them hath a diverse posture, or cringe, by themselves, which cannot but move derision in worldlings and depraved politicians, who are apt to contemn holy things.

As for the fruit towards those that are within, it is peace, which containeth infinite blessings; it establisheth faith; it kindleth charity; the outward peace of the church distilleth into peace of conscience, and it turneth the labors of writing and reading of controversies into treatises of mortification and devotion.

Concerning the bounds of unity, the true placing of them importeth exceedingly. There appear to be two extremes; for to certain zealots all speech of pacification is odious. "Is it peace, Jehu?"—"What hast thou to do with peace? turn thee behind me." Peace is not the matter, but following, and party. Contrariwise, certain Laodiceans and lukewarm persons think they may accommodate points of religion by middle ways, and taking part of both, and witty reconcilements, as if they would make an arbitrament between God and man. Both these extremes are to be avoided; which will be done if the league of Christians, penned by our Saviour himself, were in the two cross clauses thereof soundly and plainly expounded: "He that is not with us is against us;" and again, "He that is not against us, is with us;" that is, if the points fundamental, and of substance in religion, were truly discerned and distinguished from points not merely of faith, but of opinion, order, or good intention. This is a thing may seem to many a matter trivial, and done already; but if it were done less partially, it would be embraced more generally.

Of this I may give only this advice, according to my small model. Men ought to take heed of rending God's church by two kinds of controversies; the one is, when the matter of the point controverted is too small and light, not worth the heat and strife about it, kindled only by contradiction; for, as it is noted by one of the fathers, "Christ's coat indeed had no seam, but the church's vesture was of divers colors;" whereupon he saith, "In veste varietas sit, scissura non sit," they be two things, unity and uniformity; the other is, when the matter of the point controverted is great, but it is driven to an over-great subtilty and obscurity, so that it becometh a thing rather ingenious than substantial. A man that is of judgment and understanding shall sometimes hear ignorant men differ, and know well within himself, that those which so differ mean one thing, and yet they themselves would never agree; and if it come so to pass in that distance of judgment, which is between man and man, shall we not think that God above, that knows the heart, doth not discern that frail men, in some of their contradictions, intend the same thing, and accepteth of both? The nature of such controversies is excellently expressed by St. Paul, in the warning and precept that he giveth concerning the same: "Devita profanas vocum novitates, et oppositiones falsi nominis scientiæ." Men create oppositions which are not, and put them into new terms, so fixed as, whereas the meaning ought to govern the term, the term in effect governeth the meaning. There be also two false peaces, or unities; the one, when the peace is grounded but upon an implicit ignorance; for all colors will agree in the dark; the other, when it is pieced up upon a direct admission of contraries in fundamental points; for truth and falsehood, in such things, are like the iron and clay in the toes of Nebuchadnezzar's image; they may cleave, but they will not incorporate.

Concerning the means of procuring unity, men must beware that, in the procuring or muniting of religious unity, they do not dissolve and deface the laws of charity and of human society. There be two swords amongst Christians, the spiritual and temporal, and both have their due office and place in the maintenance of religion; but we may not take up the third sword, which is Mahomet's sword, or like unto it; that is, to propagate religion by wars, or, by sanguinary persecutions, to force consciences; except it be in cases of overt scandal, blasphemy, or intermixture of practice against the state; much less to nourish seditions, to authorize conspiracies and rebellions, to put the sword into the people's hands, and the like, tending to the subversion of all government, which is the ordinance of God; for this is but to dash the first table against the second, and so to consider men as Christians, as we forget that they are men. Lucretius the poet, when he beheld the act of Agamemnon, that could endure the sacrificing of his own daughter, exclaimed;—

"Tantum religio potuit suadere malorum."

What would he have said, if he had known of the massacre in France, or the powder treason of England? He would have been seven times more epicure and atheist than he was; for as the temporal sword is to be drawn with great circumspection in cases of religion, so it is a thing monstrous to put it into the hands of the common people; let that be left unto the Anabaptists, and other furies. It was great blasphemy when the devil said, "I will ascend and be like the Highest;" but it is greater blasphemy to personate God, and bring him in saying, "I will descend, and be like the prince of darkness;" and what is it better, to make the cause of religion to descend to the cruel and execrable actions of murdering princes, butchery of people, and subversion of states and governments? Surely, this is to bring down the Holy Ghost, instead of the likeness of a dove, in the shape of a vulture or raven; and to set out of the bark of a Christian church a flag of a bark of pirates and assassins; therefore, it is most necessary that the church by doctrine and decree, princes by their sword, and all learnings, both Christian and moral, as by their Mercury rod, do damn and send to hell forever those facts and opinions tending to the support of the same, as hath been already in good part done. Surely, in counsels concerning religion, that counsel of the apostle would be prefixed: "Ira hominis non implet justitiam Dei;" and it was a notable observation of a wise father, and no less ingenuously confessed, that those which held and persuaded pressure of consciences, were commonly interested therein themselves for their own ends.

Chapter 4

OF REVENGE

Revenge is a kind of wild justice, which the more man's nature runs to, the more ought law to weed it out; for as for the first wrong, it doth but offend the law, but the revenge of that wrong, putteth the law out of office. Certainly, in taking revenge, a man is but even with his enemy, but in passing it over, he is superior; for it is a prince's part to pardon; and Solomon, I am sure, saith, "It is the glory of a man to pass by an offence." That which is past is gone and irrevocable, and wise men have enough to do with things present and to come; therefore they do but trifle with themselves that labor in past matters. There is no man doth a wrong for the wrong's sake, but thereby to purchase himself profit, or pleasure, or honor, or the like; therefore, why should I be angry with a man for loving himself better than me? And if any man should do wrong merely out of ill-nature, why, yet it is but like the thorn or briar, which prick and scratch, because they can do no other. The most tolerable sort of revenge is for those wrongs which there is no law to remedy; but then, let a man take heed the revenge be such as there is no law to punish, else a man's enemy is still beforehand, and it is two for one. Some, when they take revenge, are desirous the party should know whence it cometh. This is the more generous; for the delight seemeth to be not so much in doing the hurt as in making the party repent; but base and crafty cowards are like the arrow that flieth in the dark. Cosmus, Duke of Florence, had a desperate saying against perfidious or neglecting friends, as if those wrongs were unpardonable. "You shall read," saith he, "that we are commanded to forgive our enemies; but you never read that we are commanded to forgive our friends." But yet the spirit of Job was in a better tune: "Shall we," saith he, "take good at God's hands, and not be content to take evil also?" and so of friends in a proportion. This is certain, that a man that studieth revenge keeps his own wounds green, which otherwise would heal and do well. Public revenges are for the most part fortunate; as that for the death of Cæsar; for the death of Pertinax; for the death of Henry the Third of France; and many more. But in private revenges it is not so; nay, rather, vindictive persons live the life of witches, who, as they are mischievous, so end they unfortunate.

Chapter 5

OF ADVERSITY

It was a high speech of Seneca (after the manner of the Stoics), that "the good things which belong to prosperity are to be wished, but the good things that belong to adversity are to be admired." ("Bona rerum secundarum optabilia, adversarum mirabilia.") Certainly, if miracles be the command over nature, they appear most in adversity. It is yet a higher speech of his than the other (much too high for a heathen), "It is true greatness to have in one the frailty of a man, and the security of a God." ("Vere magnum habere fragilitatem hominis securitatem Dei.") This would have done better in poesy, where transcendencies are more allowed, and the poets, indeed, have been busy with it; for it is, in effect, the thing which is figured in that strange fiction of the ancient poets, which seemeth not to be without mystery; nay, and to have some approach to the state of a Christian, "that Hercules, when he went to unbind Prometheus (by whom human nature is represented), sailed the length of the great ocean in an earthen pot or pitcher," lively describing Christian resolution, that saileth in the frail bark of the flesh through the waves of the world. But to speak in a mean, the virtue of prosperity is temperance, the virtue of adversity is fortitude, which in morals is the more heroical virtue. Prosperity is the blessing of the Old Testament, adversity is the blessing of the New, which carrieth the greater benediction, and the clearer revelation of God's favor. Yet even in the Old Testament, if you listen to David's harp, you shall hear as many hearse-like airs as carols; and the pencil of the Holy Ghost hath labored more in describing the afflictions of Job than the felicities of Solomon. Prosperity is not without many fears and distastes; and adversity is not without comforts and hopes. We see, in needleworks and embroideries, it is more pleasing to have a lively work upon a sad and solemn ground, than to have a dark and melancholy work upon a lightsome ground: judge, therefore, of the pleasure of the heart by the pleasure of the eye. Certainly, virtue is like precious odors, most fragrant when they are incensed, or crushed; for prosperity doth best discover vice, but adversity doth best discover virtue.

Chapter 6

OF SIMULATION AND DISSIMULATION

Dissimulation is but a faint kind of policy, or wisdom; for it asketh a strong wit and a strong heart to know when to tell truth, and to do it; therefore it is the weaker sort of politicians that are the great dissemblers.

Tacitus saith, "Livia sorted well with the arts of her husband, and dissimulation of her son; attributing arts or policy to Augustus, and dissimulation to Tiberius:" and again, when Mucianus encourageth Vespasian to take arms against Vitellius, he saith, "We rise not against the piercing judgment of Augustus, nor the extreme caution or closeness of Tiberius." These properties of arts or policy, and dissimulation or closeness, are indeed habits and faculties several, and to be distinguished; for if a man have that penetration of judgment as he can discern what things are to be laid open, and what to be secreted, and what to be showed at half-lights, and to whom and when (which indeed are arts of state, and arts of life, as Tacitus well calleth them), to him a habit of dissimulation is a hinderance and a poorness. But if a man cannot obtain to that judgment, then it is left to him generally to be close, and a dissembler; for where a man cannot choose or vary in particulars, there it is good to take the safest and wariest way in general, like the going softly by one that cannot well see. Certainly, the ablest men that ever were, have had all an openness and frankness of dealing, and a name of certainty and veracity: but then they were like horses well managed, for they could tell passing well when to stop or turn; and at such times, when they thought the case indeed required dissimulation, if then they used it, it came to pass that the former opinion spread abroad, of their good faith and clearness of dealing, made them almost invisible.

There be three degrees of this hiding and veiling of a man's self: the first, closeness, reservation, and secrecy; when a man leaveth himself without observation, or without hold to be taken, what he is: the second, dissimulation in the negative; when a man lets fall signs and arguments, that he is not that he is: and the third, simulation in the affirmative; when a man industriously and expressly feigns and pretends to be that he is not.

For the first of these, secrecy, it is indeed the virtue of a confessor; and assuredly the secret man heareth many confessions; for who will open himself to a blab or a babbler? But if a man be thought secret, it inviteth discovery, as the more close air sucketh in the more open; and, as in confession, the revealing is not for worldly use, but for the ease of a man's heart, so secret men come to the knowledge of many things in that kind; while men rather discharge their minds than impart their minds. In few words, mysteries are due to secrecy. Besides (to say truth), nakedness is uncomely, as well in mind as body; and it addeth no small reverence to men's manners and actions, if they be not altogether open. As for talkers and futile persons, they are commonly vain and credulous withal; for he that talketh what he knoweth, will also talk what he knoweth not; therefore set it down, that a habit of secrecy is both politic and moral: and in this part it is good that a man's face give his tongue leave to speak; for the discovery of a man's self by the tracts of his countenance, is a great weakness and betraying, by how much it is many times more marked and believed than a man's words.

For the second, which is dissimulation, it followeth many times upon secrecy by a necessity; so that he that will be secret must be a dissembler in some degree; for men are too cunning to suffer a man to keep an indifferent carriage between both, and to be secret, without swaying the balance on either side. They will so beset a man with questions, and draw him on, and pick it out of him, that without an absurd silence, he must show an inclination one way; or if he do not, they will gather as much by his silence as by his speech. As for equivocations, or oraculous speeches, they cannot hold out long: so that no man can be secret, except he give himself a little scope of dissimulation, which is, as it were, but the skirts or train of secrecy.

But for the third degree, which is simulation and false profession, that I hold more culpable, and less politic, except it be in great and rare matters; and, therefore, a general custom of simulation (which is this last degree) is a vice rising either of a natural falseness, or fearfulness, or of a mind that hath some main faults; which because a man must needs disguise, it maketh him practise simulation in other things, lest his hand should be out of use.

The advantages of simulation and dissimulation are three: first, to lay asleep opposition, and to surprise; for, where a man's intentions are published, it is an alarum to call up all that are against them: the second is, to reserve to a man's self a fair retreat; for if a man engage himself by a manifest declaration, he must go through or take a fall: the third is, the better to discover the mind of another; for to him that opens himself men will hardly show themselves adverse; but will (fair) let him go on, and turn their freedom of speech to freedom of thought; and therefore it is a good shrewd proverb of the Spaniard, "Tell a lie, and find a troth;" as if there were no way of discovery but by simulation. There be also three disadvantages to set it even; the first, that simulation and dissimulation commonly carry with them a show of fearfulness, which, in any business, doth spoil the feathers of round flying up to the mark; the second, that it puzzleth and perplexeth the conceits of many, that, perhaps, would otherwise coöperate with him, and makes a man walk almost alone to his own ends: the third, and greatest, is, that it depriveth a man of one of the most principal instruments for action, which is trust and belief. The best composition and temperature is, to have openness in fame and opinion, secrecy in habit, dissimulation in seasonable use, and a power to feign if there be no remedy.

Chapter 7

OF PARENTS AND CHILDREN

The joys of parents are secret, and so are their griefs and fears; they cannot utter the one, nor they will not utter the other. Children sweeten labors, but they make misfortunes more bitter; they increase the cares of life, but they mitigate the remembrance of death. The perpetuity by generation is common to beasts; but memory, merit, and noble works, are proper to men: and surely a man shall see the noblest works and foundations have proceeded from childless men, which have sought to express the images of their minds where those of their bodies have failed; so the care of posterity is most in them that have no posterity. They that are the first raisers of their houses are most indulgent towards their children, beholding them as the continuance, not only of their kind, but of their work; and so both children and creatures.

The difference in affection of parents towards their several children is many times unequal, and sometimes unworthy, especially in the mother; as Solomon saith, "A wise son rejoiceth the father, but an ungracious son shames the mother." A man shall see, where there is a house full of children, one or two of the eldest respected, and the youngest made wantons; but in the midst some that are, as it were, forgotten, who many times, nevertheless, prove the best. The illiberality of parents, in allowance towards their children, is a harmful error, makes them base, acquaints them with shifts, makes them sort with mean company, and makes them surfeit more when they come to plenty; and, therefore, the proof is best when men keep their authority towards their children, but not their purse. Men have a foolish manner (both parents, and schoolmasters, and servants), in creating and breeding an emulation between brothers during childhood, which many times sorteth to discord when they are men, and disturbeth families. The Italians make little difference between children and nephews, or near kinsfolk; but so they be of the lump, they care not, though they pass not through their own body; and, to say truth, in nature it is much a like matter; insomuch that we see a nephew sometimes resembleth an uncle or a kinsman more than his own parent, as the blood happens. Let parents choose betimes the vocations and courses they mean their children should take, for then they are most flexible; and let them not too much apply themselves to the disposition of their children, as thinking they will take best to that which they have most mind to. It is true, that if the affection or aptness of the children be extraordinary, then it is good not to cross it; but generally the precept is good, "Optimum elige, suave et facile illud faciet consuetudo."—Younger brothers are commonly fortunate, but seldom or never where the elder are disinherited.

Chapter 8

OF MARRIAGE AND SINGLE LIFE

H e that hath wife and children hath given hostages to fortune; for they are impediments to great enterprises, either of virtue or mischief. Certainly the best works, and of greatest merit for the public, have proceeded from the unmarried or childless men, which, both in affection and means, have married and endowed the public. Yet it were great reason that those that have children should have greatest care of future times, unto which they know they must transmit their dearest pledges. Some there are who, though they lead a single life, yet their thoughts do end with themselves, and account future times impertinences; nay, there are some other that account wife and children but as bills of charges; nay more, there are some foolish, rich, covetous men, that take a pride in having no children, because they may be thought so much the richer; for, perhaps they have heard some talk, "Such an one is a great rich man," and another except to it, "Yea, but he hath a great charge of children;" as if it were an abatement to his riches. But the most ordinary cause of a single life is liberty, especially in certain self-pleasing and humorous minds, which are so sensible of every restraint, as they will go near to think their girdles and garters to be bonds and shackles. Unmarried men are best friends, best masters, best servants; but not always best subjects, for they are light to run away, and almost all fugitives are of that condition. A single life doth well with churchmen, for charity will hardly water the ground where it must first fill a pool. It is indifferent for judges and magistrates; for if they be facile and corrupt, you shall have a servant five times worse than a wife. For soldiers, I find the generals commonly, in their hortatives, put men in mind of their wives and children; and I think the despising of marriage amongst the Turks maketh the vulgar soldier more base. Certainly, wife and children are a kind of discipline of humanity; and single men, though they be many times more charitable, because their means are less exhaust, yet, on the other side, they are more cruel and hard-hearted (good to make severe inquisitors), because their tenderness is not so oft called upon. Grave natures, led by custom, and therefore constant, are commonly loving husbands, as was said of

Ulysses, "Vetulam suam praetulit immortalitati." Chaste women are often proud and froward, as presuming upon the merit of their chastity. It is one of the best bonds, both of chastity and obedience, in the wife, if she think her husband wise, which she will never do if she find him jealous. Wives are young men's mistresses, companions for middle age, and old men's nurses, so as a man may have a quarrel to marry when he will; but yet he was reputed one of the wise men that made answer to the question when a man should marry, "A young man not yet, an elder man not at all." It is often seen that bad husbands have very good wives; whether it be that it raiseth the price of their husbands' kindness when it comes, or that the wives take a pride in their patience; but this never fails, if the bad husbands were of their own choosing, against their friends' consent, for then they will be sure to make good their own folly.

Chapter 9

OF ENVY

There be none of the affections which have been noted to fascinate or bewitch, but love and envy. They both have vehement wishes; they frame themselves readily into imaginations and suggestions, and they come easily into the eye, especially upon the presence of the objects which are the points that conduce to fascination, if any such thing there be. We see, likewise, the Scripture calleth envy an evil eye; and the astrologers call the evil influences of the stars evil aspects; so that still there seemeth to be acknowledged, in the act of envy, an exclamation, or irradiation of the eye; nay, some have been so curious as to note that the times, when the stroke or percussion of an envious eye doth most hurt, are, when the party envied is beheld in glory or triumph, for that sets an edge upon envy; and besides, at such times, the spirits of the person envied do come forth most into the outward parts, and so meet the blow.

But, leaving these curiosities (though not unworthy to be thought on in fit place), we will handle what persons are apt to envy others; what persons are most subject to be envied themselves; and what is the difference between public and private envy.

A man that hath no virtue in himself, ever envieth virtue in others; for men's minds will either feed upon their own good, or upon others' evil; and who wanteth the one will prey upon the other; and whoso is out of hope to attain to another's virtue, will seek to come at even hand by depressing another's fortune.

A man that is busy and inquisitive, is commonly envious; for to know much of other men's matters cannot be, because all that ado may concern his own estate; therefore, it must needs be that he taketh a kind of play-pleasure in looking upon the fortunes of others; neither can he that mindeth but his own business find much matter for envy; for envy is a gadding passion, and walketh the streets, and doth not keep home: "Non est curiosus, quin idem sit malevolus."

Men of noble birth are noted to be envious towards new men when they rise, for the distance is altered; and it is like a deceit of the eye, that when others come on they think themselves go back.

Deformed persons and eunuchs, and old men and bastards, are envious; for he that cannot possibly mend his own case, will do what he can to impair another's; except these defects light upon a very brave and heroical nature, which thinketh to make his natural wants part of his honor; in that it should be said, "That a eunuch, or a lame man, did such great matters," affecting the honor of a miracle; as it was in Narses the eunuch, and Agesilaus and Tamerlane, that were lame men.

The same is the case of men that rise after calamities and misfortunes; for they are as men fallen out with the times, and think other men's harms a redemption of their own sufferings.

They that desire to excel in too many matters, out of levity and vainglory, are ever envious, for they cannot want work; it being impossible but many, in some one of those things, should surpass them; which was the character of Adrian the emperor, that mortally envied poets and painters, and artificers in works, wherein he had a vein to excel.

Lastly, near kinsfolk and fellows in office, and those that have been bred together, are more apt to envy their equals when they are raised; for it doth upbraid unto them their own fortunes, and pointeth at them, and cometh oftener into their remembrance, and incurreth likewise more into the note of others; and envy ever redoubleth from speech and fame. Cain's envy was the more vile and malignant towards his brother Abel, because when his sacrifice was better accepted, there was nobody to look on. Thus much for those that are apt to envy.

Concerning those that are more or less subject to envy: First, persons of eminent virtue, when they are advanced, are less envied, for their fortune seemeth but due unto them; and no man envieth the payment of a debt, but rewards and liberality rather. Again, envy is ever joined with the comparing of a man's self; and where there is no comparison, no envy; and therefore kings are not envied but by kings. Nevertheless, it is to be noted, that unworthy persons are most envied at their first coming in, and afterwards overcome it better; whereas, contrariwise, persons of worth and merit are most envied when their fortune continueth long; for by that time, though their virtue be the same, yet it hath not the same lustre; for fresh men grow up that darken it.

Persons of noble blood are less envied in their rising; for it seemeth but right done to their birth: besides, there seemeth not so much added to their fortune; and envy is as the sunbeams, that beat hotter upon a bank or steep rising ground, than upon a flat; and, for the same reason, those that are advanced by degrees are less envied than those that are advanced suddenly, and *per saltum*.

Those that have joined with their honor great travels, cares, or perils, are less subject to envy; for men think that they earn their honors hardly, and pity them sometimes, and pity ever healeth envy. Wherefore you shall observe, that the more deep and sober sort of politic persons, in their greatness, are ever bemoaning themselves what a life they lead, chanting a *quanta patimur*; not that they feel it so, but only to abate the edge of envy; but this is to be understood of business that is laid upon men, and not such as they call unto themselves; for nothing increaseth envy more than an unnecessary and ambitious engrossing of business; and nothing doth extinguish envy more than for a great person to preserve all other inferior officers in their full rights and preëminences of their places; for, by that means, there be so many screens between him and envy.

Above all, those are most subject to envy, which carry the greatness of their fortunes in an insolent and proud manner; being never well but while they are showing how great they are, either by outward pomp, or by triumphing over all opposition or competition. Whereas wise men will rather do sacrifice to envy, in suffering themselves, sometimes of purpose, to be crossed and overborne in things that do not much concern them. Notwithstanding, so much is true, that the carriage of greatness in a plain and open manner (so it be without arrogancy and vainglory), doth draw less envy than if it be in a more crafty and cunning fashion; for in that course a man doth but disavow fortune, and seemeth to be conscious of his own want in worth, and doth but teach others to envy him.

Lastly, to conclude this part, as we said in the beginning that the act of envy had somewhat in it of witchcraft, so there is no other cure of envy but the cure of witchcraft; and that is, to remove the lot (as they call it), and to lay it upon another; for which purpose, the wiser sort of great persons bring in ever upon the stage somebody upon whom to derive the envy that would come upon themselves; sometimes upon ministers and servants, sometimes upon colleagues and associates, and the like; and, for that turn, there are never wanting some persons of violent and undertaking natures, who, so they may have power and business, will take it at any cost.

Now, to speak of public envy: there is yet some good in public envy, whereas in private there is none; for public envy is as an ostracism, that eclipseth men when they grow too great; and therefore it is a bridle also to great ones, to keep them within bounds.

This envy, being in the Latin word *invidia*, goeth in the modern languages by the name of discontentment, of which we shall speak in handling sedition. It is a disease in a state like to infection; for as infection spreadeth upon that which is sound, and tainteth it, so, when envy is gotten once into a state, it traduceth even the best actions thereof, and turneth them into an ill odor; and therefore there is little won by intermingling of plausible actions; for that doth argue but a weakness and fear of envy, which hurteth so much the more, as it is likewise usual in infections, which, if you fear them, you call them upon you.

This public envy seemeth to beat chiefly upon principal officers or ministers, rather than upon kings and estates themselves. But this is a sure rule, that if the envy upon the minister be great, when the cause of it in him is small; or if the envy be general in a manner upon all the ministers of an estate, then the envy (though hidden) is truly upon the state itself. And so much of public envy or discontentment, and the difference thereof from private envy, which was handled in the first place.

We will add this in general, touching the affection of envy, that, of all other affections, it is the most importune and continual; for of other affections there is occasion given but now and then; and therefore it was well said, "Invidia festos dies non agit:" for it is ever working upon some or other. And it is also noted, that love and envy do make a man pine, which other affections do not, because they are not so continual. It is also the vilest affection, and the most depraved; for which cause it is the proper attribute of the devil, who is called "The envious man, that soweth tares amongst the wheat by night;" as it always cometh to pass that envy worketh subtilely, and in the dark, and to the prejudice of good things, such as is the wheat.

Chapter 10

OF LOVE

The stage is more beholding to love than the life of man; for as to the stage, love is ever matter of comedies, and now and then of tragedies; but in life it doth much mischief, sometimes like a Siren, sometimes like a Fury. You may observe, that, amongst all the great and worthy persons (whereof the memory remaineth, either ancient or recent), there is not one that hath been transported to the mad degree of love, which shows that great spirits and great business do keep out this weak passion. You must except, nevertheless, Marcus Antonius, the half partner of the empire of Rome, and Appius Claudius, the decemvir and lawgiver; whereof the former was indeed a voluptuous man, and inordinate, but the latter was an austere and wise man; and therefore it seems (though rarely) that love can find entrance, not only into an open heart, but also into a heart well fortified, if watch be not well kept. It is a poor saying of Epicurus, "Satis magnum alter alteri theatrum sumus;" as if man, made for the contemplation of heaven and all noble objects, should do nothing but kneel before a little idol, and make himself subject, though not of the mouth (as beasts are) yet of the eye, which was given him for higher purposes. It is a strange thing to note the excess of this passion, and how it braves the nature and value of things, by this, that the speaking in a perpetual hyperbole is comely in nothing but in love, neither is it merely in the phrase; for whereas it hath been well said, "That the arch flatterer, with whom all the petty flatterers have intelligence, is a man's self;" certainly, the lover is more; for there was never proud man thought so absurdly well of himself as the lover doth of the person loved; and therefore it was well said, "That it is impossible to love and to be wise." Neither doth this weakness appear to others only, and not to the party loved, but to the loved most of all, except the love be reciprocal; for it is a true rule, that love is ever rewarded, either with the reciprocal, or with an inward and secret contempt; by how much the more men ought to beware of this passion, which loseth not only other things, but itself. As for the other losses, the poet's relation doth well figure them: "That he that preferred Helena, quitted the gifts of Juno and Pallas;" for whosoever esteemeth too much of amorous affection, quitteth both riches and wisdom. This passion hath his floods in the very times of weakness, which are, great prosperity and great adversity, though this latter hath been less observed; both which times kindle love, and make it more fervent, and therefore show it to be the child of folly. They do best who, if they cannot but admit love, yet make it keep quarter, and sever it wholly from their serious affairs and actions of life; for if it check once with business, it troubleth men's fortunes, and maketh men that they can nowise be true to their own ends. I know not how, but martial men are given to love; I think it is, but as they are given to wine, for perils commonly ask to be paid in pleasures. There is in man's nature a secret inclination and motion towards love of others, which, if it be not spent upon some one or a few, doth naturally spread itself towards many, and maketh men become humane and charitable, as it is seen sometimes in friars. Nuptial love maketh mankind, friendly love perfecteth it, but wanton love corrupted and embaseth it.

Chapter 11

OF GREAT PLACE

M en in great place are thrice servants—servants of the sovereign or state, servants of fame, and servants of business; so as they have no freedom, neither in their persons, nor in their actions, nor in their times. It is a strange desire to seek power and to lose liberty; or to seek power over others, and to lose power over a man's self. The rising unto place is laborious, and by pains men come to greater pains; and it is sometimes base, and by indignities men come to dignities. The standing is slippery, and the regress is either a downfall, or at least an eclipse, which is a melancholy thing: "Cum non sis qui fueris, non esse cur velis vivere." Nay, retire men cannot when they would, neither will they when it were reason; but are impatient of privateness even in age and sickness, which require the shadow; like old townsmen, that will be still sitting at their street door, though thereby they offer age to scorn. Certainly, great persons had need to borrow other men's opinions to think themselves happy; for if they judge by their own feeling, they cannot find it; but if they think with themselves what other men think of them, and that other men would fain be as they are, then they are happy as it were by report, when, perhaps, they find the contrary within; for they are the first that find their own griefs, though they be the last that find their own faults. Certainly, men in great fortunes are strangers to themselves, and while they are in the puzzle of business, they have no time to tend their health either of body or mind.

> *"Illi mors gravis incubat,*
> *Qui notus nimis omnibus,*
> *Ignotus moritur."*

In place, there is license to do good and evil, whereof the latter is a curse; for in evil, the best condition is not to will, the second not to can. But power to do good is the true and lawful end of aspiring; for good thoughts, though God accept them, yet towards men are little better than good dreams, except they be put in act; and that cannot be without power and place, as the vantage and commanding ground. Merit and good works are the end of man's motion, and conscience of the same is the accomplishment of man's rest; for if a man can be partaker of God's theatre, he shall likewise be partaker of God's rest. "Et conversus Deus, ut aspiceret opera, quæ fecerunt manus suæ, vidit quod omnia essent bona nimis;" and then the Sabbath.

In the discharge of thy place, set before thee the best examples; for imitation is a globe of precepts, and after a time set before thee thine own example; and examine thyself strictly whether thou didst not best at first. Neglect not also the examples of those that have carried themselves ill in the same place; not to set off thyself by taxing their memory, but to direct thyself what to avoid. Reform, therefore, without bravery or scandal of former times and persons; but yet set it down to thyself, as well to create good precedents as to follow them. Reduce things to the first institution, and observe wherein and how they have degenerated; but yet ask counsel of both times—of the ancient time what is best, and of the latter time what is fittest. Seek to make thy course regular, that men may know beforehand what they may expect; but be not too positive and peremptory, and express thyself well when thou digressest from thy rule. Preserve the right of thy place, but stir not questions of jurisdiction; and rather assume thy right in silence, and *de facto*, than voice it with claims and challenges. Preserve likewise the rights of inferior places; and think it more honor to direct in chief than to be busy in all. Embrace and invite helps and advices touching the execution of thy place; and do not drive away such as bring thee information, as meddlers, but accept of them in good part. The vices of authority are chiefly four: delays, corruption, roughness, and facility. For delays, give easy access, keep times appointed, go through with that which is in hand, and interlace not business but of necessity. For corruption, do not only bind thine own hands or thy servant's hands from taking, but bind the hands of suitors also from offering; for integrity used doth the one, but integrity professed, and with a manifest detestation of bribery, doth the other; and avoid not only the fault, but the suspicion. Whosoever is found variable, and changeth manifestly without manifest cause, giveth suspicion of corruption; therefore, always when thou changest thine opinion or course, profess it plainly, and declare it, together with the reasons that move thee to change, and do not think to steal it. A servant or a favorite, if he be inward, and no other apparent cause of esteem, is commonly thought but a by-way to close corruption. For roughness, it is a needless cause of discontent: severity breedeth fear, but roughness breedeth hate. Even reproofs from authority ought to be grave, and not taunting. As for facility, it is worse than bribery, for bribes come but now and then; but if importunity or idle respects lead a man, he shall never be without; as Solomon saith, "To respect persons is not good; for such a man will transgress for a piece of bread."

It is most true that was anciently spoken: "A place showeth the man; and it showeth some to the better, and some to the worse:" "Omnium consensu capax imperii, nisi imperasset," saith Tacitus of Galba; but of Vespasian he saith, "Solus imperantium, Vespasianus mutatus in melius;" though the one was meant of sufficiency, the other of manners and affection. It is an assured sign of a worthy and generous spirit, whom honor amends; for honor is, or should be, the place of virtue; and as in nature things move violently to their place, and calmly in their place, so virtue in ambition is violent, in authority settled and calm. All rising to great place is by a winding stair; and if there be factions, it is good to side a man's self whilst he is in the rising, and to balance himself when he is placed. Use the memory of thy predecessor fairly and tenderly; for if thou dost not, it is a debt will sure be paid when thou art gone. If thou have colleagues, respect them; and rather call them when they look not for it, than exclude them when they have reason to look to be called. Be not too sensible or too remembering of thy place in conversation and private answers to suitors; but let it rather be said, "When he sits in place, he is another man."

Chapter 12

OF BOLDNESS

It is a trivial grammar-school text, but yet worthy a wise man's consideration. Question was asked of Demosthenes, what was the chief part of an orator? He answered, Action. What next?—Action. What next again?—Action. He said it that knew it best, and had, by nature, himself no advantage in that he commended. A strange thing, that that part of an orator which is but superficial, and rather the virtue of a player, should be placed so high above those other noble parts of invention, elocution, and the rest; nay, almost alone, as if it were all in all. But the reason is plain. There is in human nature generally more of the fool than of the wise; and therefore, those faculties by which the foolish part of men's minds is taken are most potent. Wonderful like is the case of boldness in civil business. What first?—Boldness: what second and third?—Boldness. And yet boldness is a child of ignorance and baseness, far inferior to other parts; but, nevertheless, it doth fascinate, and bind hand and foot those that are either shallow in judgment or weak in courage, which are the greatest part, yea, and prevaileth with wise man at weak times; therefore, we see it hath done wonders in popular states, but with senates and princes less, and more, ever upon the first entrance of bold persons into action than soon after; for boldness is an ill keeper of promise. Surely, as there are mountebanks for the natural body, so are there mountebanks for the politic body; men that undertake great cures, and perhaps have been lucky in two or three experiments, but want the grounds of science, and therefore cannot hold out; nay, you shall see a bold fellow many times do Mahomet's miracle. Mahomet made the people believe that he would call a hill to him, and from the top of it offer up his prayers for the observers of his law. The people assembled; Mahomet called the hill to come to him again and again; and when the hill stood still, he was never a whit abashed, but said, "If the hill will not come to Mahomet, Mahomet will go to the hill." So these men, when they have promised great matters and failed most shamefully, yet, if they have the perfection of boldness, they will but slight it over, and make a turn, and no more ado. Certainly, to men of great judgment, bold persons are a sport to behold; nay, and to the vulgar also boldness hath somewhat of the ridiculous; for if absurdity be the subject of laughter, doubt you not but great boldness is seldom without some absurdity; especially it is a sport to see when a bold fellow is out of countenance, for that puts his face into a most shrunken and wooden posture, as needs it must; for in bashfulness the spirits do a little go and come, but with bold men, upon like occasion, they stand at a stay; like a stale at chess, where it is no mate, but yet the game cannot stir; but this last were fitter for a satire than for a serious observation. This is well to be weighed, that boldness is ever blind, for it seeth not dangers and inconveniences; therefore, it is ill in counsel, good in execution; so that the right use of bold persons is, that they never command in chief, but be seconds and under the direction of others; for in counsel it is good to see dangers; and in execution not to see them except they be very great.

Chapter 13

OF GOODNESS, AND GOODNESS OF NATURE

I take goodness in this sense, the affecting of the weal of men, which is that the Grecians call *philanthropia*; and the word humanity, as it is used, is a little too light to express it. Goodness I call the habit, and goodness of nature the inclination. This, of all virtues and dignities of the mind, is the greatest, being the character of the Deity; and without it man is a busy, mischievous, wretched thing, no better than a kind of vermin. Goodness answers to the theological virtue charity, and admits no excess but error. The desire of power in excess caused the angels to fall; the desire of knowledge in excess caused man to fall; but in charity there is no excess, neither can angel or man come in danger by it. The inclination to goodness is imprinted deeply in the nature of man, insomuch that if it issue not towards men, it will take unto other living creatures; as it is seen in the Turks, a cruel people, who nevertheless are kind to beasts, and give alms to dogs and birds; insomuch, as Busbechius reporteth, a Christian boy in Constantinople had like to have been stoned for gagging in a waggishness a long-billed fowl. Errors, indeed, in this virtue, of goodness or charity, may be committed. The Italians have an ungracious proverb: "Tanto buon che val niente;" "So good, that he is good for nothing;" and one of the doctors of Italy, Nicholas Machiavel, had the confidence to put in writing, almost in plain terms, "That the Christian faith had given up good men in prey to those that are tyrannical and unjust;" which he spake, because, indeed, there was never law, or sect, or opinion did so much magnify goodness as the Christian religion doth; therefore, to avoid the scandal and the danger both, it is good to take knowledge of the errors of a habit so excellent. Seek the good of other men, but be not in bondage to their faces or fancies; for that is but facility or softness, which taketh an honest mind prisoner. Neither give thou Æsop's cock a gem, who would be better pleased and happier if he had had a barley-corn. The example of God teacheth the lesson truly: "He sendeth his rain, and maketh his sun to shine upon the just and the unjust;" but he doth not rain wealth, nor shine honor and virtues upon men equally; common benefits are to be communicate with all, but peculiar benefits with choice. And beware how, in making the portraiture, thou breakest the pattern; for divinity maketh the love of ourselves the pattern, the love of our neighbors but the portraiture: "Sell all thou hast, and give it to the poor, and follow me;" but sell not all thou hast, except thou come and follow me; that is, except thou have a vocation wherein thou mayest do as much good with little means as with great; for otherwise, in feeding the streams thou driest the fountain. Neither is there only a habit of goodness directed by right reason, but there is in some men, even in nature, a disposition towards it; as, on the other side, there is a natural malignity, for there be that in their nature do not affect the good of others. The lighter sort of malignity turneth but to a crossness, or frowardness, or aptness to oppose, or difficileness, or the like; but the deeper sort to envy, and mere mischief. Such men in other men's calamities are, as it were, in season, and are ever on the loading part; not so good as the dogs that licked Lazarus's sores, but like flies that are still buzzing upon any thing that is raw; misanthropi, that make it their practice to bring men to the bough, and yet have never a tree for the purpose in their gardens, as Timon had. Such dispositions are the very errors of human nature, and yet they are the fittest timber to make great politics of; like to knee timber, that is good for ships that are ordained to be tossed, but not for building houses that shall stand firm. The parts and signs of goodness are many. If a man be gracious and courteous to strangers, it shows he is a citizen of the world, and that his heart is no island cut off from other lands, but a continent that joins to them; if he be compassionate towards the afflictions of others, it shows that his heart is like the noble tree that is wounded itself when it gives the balm; if he easily pardons and remits offences, it shows that his mind is planted above injuries, so that he cannot be shot; if he be thankful for small benefits, it shows that he weighs men's minds, and not their trash; but, above all, if he have St. Paul's perfection, that he would wish to be an anathema from Christ for the salvation of his brethren, it shows much of a divine nature, and a kind of conformity with Christ himself.

Chapter 14

OF NOBILITY

We will speak of nobility, first, as a portion of an estate, then as a condition of particular persons. A monarchy, where there is no nobility at all, is ever a pure and absolute tyranny as that of the Turks; for nobility attempers sovereignty, and draws the eyes of the people somewhat aside from the line royal: but for democracies they need it not; and they are commonly more quiet and less subject to sedition than where there are stirps of nobles; for men's eyes are upon the business, and not upon the persons; or if upon the persons, it is for the business sake, as fittest, and not for flags and pedigree. We see the Switzers last well, notwithstanding their diversity of religion and of cantons; for utility is their bond, and not respects. The United Provinces of the Low Countries in their government excel; for where there is an equality the consultations are more indifferent, and the payments and tributes more cheerful. A great and potent nobility addeth majesty to a monarch, but diminisheth power, and putteth life and spirit into the people, but presseth their fortune. It is well when nobles are not too great for sovereignty nor for justice; and yet maintained in that height, as the insolency of inferiors may be broken upon them, before it come on too fast upon the majesty of kings. A numerous nobility causeth poverty and inconvenience in a state, for it is a surcharge of expense; and besides, it being of necessity that many of the nobility fall in time to be weak in fortune, it maketh a kind of disproportion between honor and means.

As for nobility in particular persons, it is a reverend thing to see an ancient castle or building not in decay, or to see a fair timber-tree sound and perfect; how much more to behold an ancient noble family, which hath stood against the waves and weathers of time! For new nobility is but the act of power, but ancient nobility is the act of time. Those that are first raised to nobility are commonly more virtuous, but less innocent than their descendants; for there is rarely any rising but by a commixture of good and evil arts; but it is reason the memory of their virtues remain to their posterity, and their faults die with themselves. Nobility of birth commonly abateth industry, and he that is not industrious, envieth him that is; besides, noble persons cannot go much higher; and he that standeth at a stay when others rise, can hardly avoid motions of envy. On the other side, nobility extinguisheth the passive envy from others towards them, because they are in possession of honor. Certainly, kings that have able men of their nobility shall find ease in employing them, and a better slide into their business; for people naturally bend to them, as born in some sort to command.

Chapter 15

OF SEDITIONS AND TROUBLES

Shepherds of people had need know the calendars of tempests in state, which are commonly greatest when things grow to equality; as natural tempests are greatest about the equinoctia, and as there are certain hollow blasts of wind and secret swellings of seas before a tempest, so are there in states:—

> *"Ille etiam cæcos instare tumultus*
> *Sæpe monet, fraudesque et operta tumescere bella."*

Libels and licentious discourses against the state, when they are frequent and open; and in like sort false news, often running up and down, to the disadvantage of the state, and hastily embraced, are amongst the signs of troubles. Virgil, giving the pedigree of Fame, saith she was sister to the giants:—

> *"Illam Terra parens, irâ irritata Deorum,*
> *Extremam (ut perhibent) Cœo Enceladoque sororem*
> *Progenuit."*

As if fames were the relics of seditions past; but they are no less indeed the preludes of seditions to come. Howsoever, he noteth it right, that seditious tumults and seditious fames differ no more but as brother and sister, masculine and feminine; especially if it come to that, that the best actions of a state, and the most plausible, and which ought to give greatest contentment, are taken in ill sense, and traduced; for that shows the envy great, as Tacitus saith, "Conflatâ magnâ, invidiâ, seu bene, seu male, gesta premunt." Neither doth it follow, that because these fames are a sign of troubles, that the suppressing of them with too much severity should be a remedy of troubles; for the despising of them many times checks them best, and the going about to stop them doth but make a wonder long-lived. Also that kind of obedience, which Tacitus speaketh of, is to be held suspected: "Erant in officio, sed tamen qui mallent imperantium mandata interpretari, quam exsequi;"

disputing, excusing, cavilling upon mandates and directions, is a kind of shaking off the yoke, and assay of disobedience; especially if, in those disputings, they which are for the direction speak fearfully and tenderly, and those that are against it audaciously.

Also, as Machiavel noteth well, when princes, that ought to be common parents, make themselves as a party, and lean to a side; it is as a boat that is overthrown by uneven weight on the one side, as was well seen in the time of Henry the Third of France; for first himself entered league for the extirpation of the Protestants, and presently after the same league was turned upon himself; for when the authority of princes is made but an accessary to a cause, and that there be other bands that tie faster than the band of sovereignty, kings begin to be put almost out of possession.

Also, when discords, and quarrels, and factions are carried openly and audaciously, it is a sign the reverence of government is lost; for the motions of the greatest persons in a government ought to be as the motions of the planets under "primum mobile," according to the old opinion, which is, that every of them is carried swiftly by the highest motion, and softly in their own motion; and therefore, when great ones in their own particular motion move violently, and as Tacitus expresseth it well, "liberius quam ut imperantium meminissent," it is a sign the orbs are out of frame; for reverence is that wherewith princes are girt from God, who threateneth the dissolving thereof: "Solvam cingula regum."

So when any of the four pillars of government are mainly shaken or weakened (which are religion, justice, counsel, and treasure), men had need to pray for fair weather. But let us pass from this part of predictions (concerning which, nevertheless, more light may be taken from that which followeth), and let us speak first of the materials of seditions; then of the motives of them; and thirdly of the remedies.

Concerning the materials of seditions, it is a thing well to be considered, for the surest way to prevent seditions (if the times do bear it), is to take away the matter of them; for if there be fuel prepared, it is hard to tell whence the spark shall come that shall set it on fire. The matter of seditions is of two kinds, much poverty and much discontentment. It is certain, so many overthrown estates, so many votes for troubles. Lucan noteth well the state of Rome before the civil war:—

> *"Hinc usura vorax, rapidumque in tempore fœnus,*
> *Hinc concussa fides, et multis utile bellum."*

This same "multis utile bellum," is an assured and infallible sign of a state disposed to seditions and troubles; and if this poverty and broken estate in the better sort be joined with a want and necessity in the mean people, the danger is imminent and great; for the rebellions of the belly are the worst. As for discontentments, they are in the politic body like to humors in the natural, which are apt to gather a preternatural heat and to inflame; and let no prince measure the danger of them by this, whether they be just or unjust; for that were to imagine people to be too reasonable, who do often spurn at their own good; nor yet by this, whether the griefs whereupon they rise be in fact great or small; for they are the most dangerous discontentments where the fear is greater than the feeling: "Dolendi modus, timendi non item." Besides, in great oppressions, the same things that provoke the patience, do withal mate the courage; but in fears it is not so; neither let any prince or state be secure concerning discontentments, because they have been often or have been long, and yet no peril hath ensued; for as it is true that every vapor or fume doth not turn into a storm, so it is nevertheless true that storms, though they blow over divers times, yet may fall at last; and, as the Spanish proverb noteth well, "The cord breaketh at the last by the weakest pull."

The causes and motives of seditions are, innovation in religion, taxes, alteration of laws and customs, breaking of privileges, general oppression, advancement of unworthy persons, strangers, dearths, disbanded soldiers, factions grown desperate, and whatsoever in offending people joineth and knitteth them in a common cause.

For the remedies, there may be some general preservatives, whereof we will speak; as for the just cure, it must answer to the particular disease, and so be left to counsel rather than rule.

The first remedy, or prevention, is to remove, by all means possible, that material cause of sedition whereof we spake, which is, want and poverty in the estate; to which purpose serveth the opening and well-balancing of trade; the cherishing of manufactures; the banishing of idleness; the repressing of waste and excess by sumptuary laws; the improvement and husbanding of the soil; the regulating of prices of things vendible; the moderating of taxes and tributes, and the like. Generally, it is to be foreseen that the population of a kingdom (especially if it be not mown down by wars) do not exceed the stock of the kingdom which should maintain them; neither is the population to be reckoned only by number; for a smaller number, that spend more and earn less, do wear out an estate sooner than a greater number that live lower and gather more. Therefore the multiplying of nobility and other degrees of quality, in an over-proportion to the common people, doth speedily bring a state to necessity; and so doth likewise an overgrown clergy, for they bring nothing to the stock; and in like manner, when more are bred scholars than preferments can take off.

It is likewise to be remembered, that, forasmuch as the increase of any estate must be upon the foreigner (for whatsoever is somewhere gotten is somewhere lost), there be but three things which one nation selleth unto another; the commodity, as nature yieldeth it; the manufacture; and the vecture, or carriage; so that, if these three wheels go, wealth will flow as in a spring tide. And it cometh many times to pass, that, "materiam superabit opus," that the work and carriage is more worth than the material, and enricheth a state more; as is notably seen in the Low Countrymen, who have the best mines above ground in the world.

Above all things, good policy is to be used, that the treasure and moneys in a state be not gathered into few hands; for, otherwise, a state may have a great stock, and yet starve. And money is like muck, not good except it be spread. This is done chiefly by suppressing, or, at the least, keeping a strait hand upon the devouring trades of usury, engrossing great pasturages, and the like.

For removing discontentments, or, at least, the danger of them, there is in every state (as we know) two portions of subjects, the nobles and the commonalty. When one of these is discontent, the danger is not great; for common people are of slow motion, if they be not excited by the greater sort; and the greater sort are of small strength, except the multitude be apt and ready to move of themselves; then is the danger, when the greater sort do but wait for the troubling of the waters amongst the meaner, that then they may declare themselves. The poets feign that the rest of the gods would have bound Jupiter, which he hearing of, by the counsel of Pallas, sent for Briareus, with his hundred hands, to come in to his aid; an emblem, no doubt, to show how safe it is for monarchs to make sure of the good-will of common people.

To give moderate liberty for griefs and discontentments to evaporate (so it be without too great insolency or bravery), is a safe way; for he that turneth the humors back, and maketh the wound bleed inwards, endangereth malign ulcers and pernicious imposthumations.

The part of Epimetheus might well become Prometheus, in the case of discontentments, for there is not a better provision against them.

Epimetheus, when griefs and evils flew abroad, at last shut the lid, and kept Hope in the bottom of the vessel. Certainly, the politic and artificial nourishing and entertaining of hopes, and carrying men from hopes to hopes, is one of the best antidotes against the poison of discontentments; and it is a certain sign of a wise government and proceeding, when it can hold men's hearts by hopes, when it cannot by satisfaction; and when it can handle things in such manner as no evil shall appear so peremptory, but that it hath some outlet of hope; which is the less hard to do, because both particular persons and factions are apt enough to flatter themselves, or at least to brave that which they believe not.

Also the foresight and prevention, that there be no likely or fit head whereunto discontented persons may resort, and under whom they may join, is a known but an excellent point of caution. I understand a fit head to be one that hath greatness and reputation, that hath confidence with the discontented party, and upon whom they turn their eyes, and that is thought discontented in his own particular: which kind of persons are either to be won and reconciled to the state, and that in a fast and true manner; or to be fronted with some other of the same party that may oppose them, and so divide the reputation. Generally, the dividing and breaking of all factions and combinations that are adverse to the state, and setting them at distance, or, at least, distrust amongst themselves, is not one of the worst remedies; for it is a desperate case, if those that hold with the proceeding of the state be full of discord and faction, and those that are against it be entire and united.

I have noted, that some witty and sharp speeches, which have fallen from princes, have given fire to seditions. Cæsar did himself infinite hurt in that speech—"Sylla nescivit literas, non potuit dictare," for it did utterly cut off that hope which men had entertained, that he would, at one time or other, give over his dictatorship. Galba undid himself by that speech, "Legi a se militem, non emi;" for it put the soldiers out of hope of the donative. Probus, likewise, by that speech, "Si vixero, non opus erit amplius Romano imperio militibus;" a speech of great despair for the soldiers, and many the like. Surely princes had need, in tender matters and ticklish times, to beware what they say, especially in these short speeches, which fly abroad like darts, and are thought to be shot out of their secret intentions; for as for large discourses, they are flat things, and not so much noted.

Lastly, let princes, against all events, not be without some great person, one or rather more, of military valor, near unto them, for the repressing of seditions in their beginnings; for without that, there useth to be more trepidation in court upon the first breaking out of troubles than were fit, and the state runneth the danger of that which Tacitus saith: "Atque is habitus animorum fuit, ut pessimum facinus auderent pauci, plures vellent, omnes paterentur:" but let such military persons be assured, and well reputed of, rather than factious and popular; holding also good correspondence with the other great men in the state, or else the remedy is worse than the disease.

Chapter 16

OF ATHEISM

I had rather believe all the fables in the legends, and the Talmud, and the Alcoran, than that this universal frame is without a mind; and, therefore, God never wrought miracle to convince atheism, because his ordinary works convince it. It is true, that a little philosophy inclineth man's mind to atheism, but depth in philosophy bringeth men's minds about to religion; for while the mind of man looketh upon second causes scattered, it may sometimes rest in them, and go no further; but when it beholdeth the chain of them confederate, and linked together, it must needs fly to Providence and Deity. Nay, even that school which is most accused of atheism, doth most demonstrate religion: that is, the school of Leucippus, and Democritus, and Epicurus; for it is a thousand times more credible that four mutable elements, and one immutable fifth essence, duly and eternally placed, need no God, than that an army of infinite small portions, or seeds unplaced, should have produced this order and beauty without a divine marshal. The Scripture saith, "The fool hath said in his heart, there is no God;" it is not said, "The fool hath thought in his heart;" so as he rather saith it by rote to himself, as that he would have, than that he can thoroughly believe it, or be persuaded of it; for none deny there is a God, but those for whom it maketh that there were no God. It appeareth in nothing more, that atheism is rather in the lip than in the heart of man, than by this, that atheists will ever be talking of that their opinion, as if they fainted in it within themselves, and would be glad to be strengthened by the consent of others; nay more, you shall have atheists strive to get disciples, as it fareth with other sects; and, which is most of all, you shall have of them that will suffer for atheism, and not recant; whereas, if they did truly think that there were no such thing as God, why should they trouble themselves? Epicurus is charged, that he did but dissemble for his credit's sake, when he affirmed there were blessed natures, but such as enjoyed themselves without having respect to the government of the world. Wherein they say he did temporize, though in secret he thought there was no God; but certainly he is traduced, for his words are noble and divine: "Non Deos vulgi negare profanum; sed vulgi opiniones Diis applicare profanum." Plato could have said no more; and, although he had the confidence to deny the administration, he had not the power to deny the nature. The Indians of the west have names for their particular gods, though they have no name for God; as if the heathens should have had the names Jupiter, Apollo, Mars, &c., but not the word Deus, which shows that even those barbarous people have the notion, though they have not the latitude and extent of it; so that against atheists the very savages take part with the very subtlest philosophers. The contemplative atheist is rare; a Diagoras, a Bion, a Lucian, perhaps, and some others, and yet they seem to be more than they are; for that all that impugn a received religion, or superstition, are, by the adverse part, branded with the name of atheists. But the great atheists indeed are hypocrites, which are ever handling holy things, but without feeling, so as they must needs be cauterized in the end. The causes of atheism are: divisions in religion, if they be many; for any one main division addeth zeal to both sides, but many divisions introduce atheism. Another is, scandal of priests, when it is come to that which St. Bernard saith: "Non est jam dicere, ut populus, sic sacerdos; quia nec sic populus, ut sacerdos." A third is, custom of profane scoffing in holy matters, which doth by little and little deface the reverence of religion: and lastly, learned times, specially with peace and prosperity; for troubles and adversities do more bow men's minds to religion. They that deny a God destroy a man's nobility, for certainly man is of kin to the beasts by his body; and if he be not of kin to God by his spirit, he is a base and ignoble creature. It destroys likewise magnanimity, and the raising of human nature; for, take an example of a dog, and mark what a generosity and courage he will put on when he finds himself maintained by a man, who, to him, is instead of a God, or "melior natura;" which courage is manifestly such as that creature, without that confidence of a better nature than his own, could never attain. So man, when he resteth and assureth himself upon divine protection and favor, gathereth a force and faith, which human nature in itself could not obtain; therefore, as atheism is in all respects hateful, so in this, that it depriveth human nature of the means to exalt itself above human frailty. As it is in particular persons, so it is in nations: never was there such a state for magnanimity as Rome. Of this state hear what Cicero saith: "Quam volumus, licet, Patres conscripti, nos amemus, tamen nec numero Hispanos, nec robore Gallos, nec calliditate Pœnos, nec artibus Græcos, nec denique hoc ipso hujus gentis et terræ domestico nativoque sensu Italos ipsos et Latinos; sed pietate, ac religione, atque hâc unâ sapientiâ, quod Deorum immortalium numine omnia regi, gubernarique perspeximus, omnes gentes, nationesque superavimus."

Chapter 17

OF SUPERSTITION

It were better to have no opinion of God at all, than such an opinion as is unworthy of him; for the one is unbelief, the other is contumely, and certainly superstition is the reproach of the Deity. Plutarch saith well to that purpose: "Surely," saith he, "I had rather a great deal men should say there was no such man at all as Plutarch, than that they should say that there was one Plutarch that would eat his children as soon as they were born," as the poets speak of Saturn; and, as the contumely is greater towards God, so the danger is greater towards men. Atheism leaves a man to sense, to philosophy, to natural piety, to laws, to reputation, all which may be guides to an outward moral virtue, though religion were not; but superstition dismounts all these, and erecteth an absolute monarchy in the minds of men. Therefore atheism did never perturb states; for it makes men wary of themselves, as looking no further, and we see the times inclined to atheism (as the time of Augustus Cæsar) were civil times; but superstition hath been the confusion of many states, and bringeth in a new *primum mobile*, that ravisheth all the spheres of government. The master of superstition is the people, and in all superstition wise men follow fools; and arguments are fitted to practice in a reversed order. It was gravely said by some of the prelates in the Council of Trent, where the doctrine of the schoolmen bare great sway, that the schoolmen were like astronomers, which did feign eccentrics and epicycles, and such engines of orbs to save the phenomena, though they knew there were no such things; and, in like manner, that the schoolmen had framed a number of subtle and intricate axioms and theorems, to save the practice of the Church. The causes of superstition are, pleasing and sensual rites and ceremonies; excess of outward and pharisaical holiness; over-great reverence of traditions, which cannot but load the Church; the stratagems of prelates for their own ambition and lucre; the favoring too much of good intentions, which openeth the gate to conceits and novelties; the taking an aim at divine matters by human, which cannot but breed mixture of imaginations; and, lastly, barbarous times, especially joined with calamities and disasters. Superstition, without a veil, is a deformed thing; for, as it addeth deformity to an ape to be so like a man, so the similitude of superstition to religion makes it the more deformed; and as wholesome meat corrupteth to little worms, so good forms and orders corrupt into a number of petty observances. There is a superstition in avoiding superstition, when men think to do best if they go furthest from the superstition formerly received; therefore care would be had that (as it fareth in ill purgings) the good be not taken away with the bad, which commonly is done when the people is the reformer.

Chapter 18

OF TRAVEL

Travel, in the younger sort, is a part of education; in the elder, a part of experience. He that travelleth into a country before he hath some entrance into the language, goeth to school, and not to travel. That young men travel under some tutor or grave servant, I allow well, so that he be such a one that hath the language, and hath been in the country before; whereby he may be able to tell them what things are worthy to be seen in the country where they go, what acquaintances they are to seek, what exercises or discipline the place yieldeth; for else young men shall go hooded, and look abroad little. It is a strange thing that, in sea voyages, where there is nothing to be seen but sky and sea, men should make diaries; but in land travel, wherein so much is to be observed, for the most part they omit it, as if chance were fitter to be registered than observation. Let diaries, therefore, be brought in use. The things to be seen and observed are, the courts of princes, especially when they give audience to ambassadors; the courts of justice, while they sit and hear causes; and so of consistories ecclesiastic; the churches and monasteries, with the monuments which are therein extant; the walls and fortifications of cities and towns; and so the havens and harbors, antiquities and ruins, libraries, colleges, disputations, and lectures, where any are; shipping and navies; houses and gardens of state and pleasure, near great cities; armories, arsenals, magazines, exchanges, burses, warehouses, exercises of horsemanship, fencing, training of soldiers, and the like; comedies, such whereunto the better sort of persons do resort; treasuries of jewels and robes; cabinets and rarities; and, to conclude, whatsoever is memorable in the places where they go, after all which the tutors or servants ought to make diligent inquiry. As for triumphs, masks, feasts, weddings, funerals, capital executions, and such shows, men need not to be put in mind of them; yet they are not to be neglected. If you will have a young man to put his travel into a little room, and in short time to gather much, this you must do: first, as was said, he must have some entrance into the language before he goeth; then he must have such a servant, or tutor, as knoweth the country, as was likewise said; let him carry with him also some card or book, describing the country where he travelleth, which will be a good key to his inquiry; let him keep also a diary; let him not stay long in one city or town, more or less, as the place deserveth, but not long; nay, when he stayeth in one city or town, let him change his lodging from one end and part of the town to another, which is a great adamant of acquaintance; let him sequester himself from the company of his countrymen, and diet in such places where there is good company of the nation where he travelleth; let him, upon his removes from one place to another, procure recommendation to some person of quality residing in the place whither he removeth, that he may use his favor in those things he desireth to see or know: thus he may abridge his travel with much profit. As for the acquaintance which is to be sought in travel, that which is most of all profitable, is acquaintance with the secretaries and employed men of ambassadors, for so in travelling in one country he shall suck the experience of many; let him also see and visit eminent persons in all kinds which are of great name abroad, that he may be able to tell how the life agreeth with the fame. For quarrels, they are with care and discretion to be avoided; they are commonly for mistresses, healths, place, and words; and let a man beware how he keepeth company with choleric and quarrelsome persons, for they will engage him into their own quarrels. When a traveller returneth home, let him not leave the countries where he hath travelled altogether behind him, but maintain a correspondence by letters with those of his acquaintance which are of most worth; and let his travel appear rather in his discourse than in his apparel or gesture, and in his discourse let him be rather advised in his answers, than forward to tell stories; and let it appear that he doth not change his country manners for those of foreign parts, but only prick in some flowers of that he hath learned abroad into the customs of his own country.

Chapter 19

Of Empire

It is a miserable state of mind to have few things to desire, and many things to fear; and yet that commonly is the case of kings, who, being, at the highest, want matter of desire, which makes their minds more languishing; and have many representations of perils and shadows, which makes their minds the less clear; and this is one reason, also, of that effect which the Scripture speaketh of, "that the king's heart is inscrutable;" for multitude of jealousies, and lack of some predominant desire, that should marshal and put in order all the rest, maketh any man's heart hard to find or sound. Hence it comes, likewise, that princes many times make themselves desires, and set their hearts upon toys: sometimes upon a building; sometimes upon erecting of an order; sometimes upon the advancing of a person; sometimes upon obtaining excellency in some art or feat of the hand,—as Nero for playing on the harp; Domitian for certainty of the hand with the arrow; Commodus for playing at fence; Caracalla for driving chariots, and the like. This seemeth incredible unto those that know not the principle, that the mind of man is more cheered and refreshed by profiting in small things than by standing at a stay in great. We see, also, that kings that have been fortunate conquerors in their first years, it being not possible for them to go forward infinitely, but that they must have some check or arrest in their fortunes, turn in their latter years to be superstitious and melancholy; as did Alexander the Great, Diocletian, and, in our memory, Charles the Fifth, and others; for he that is used to go forward, and findeth a stop, falleth out of his own favor, and is not the thing he was.

To speak now of the true temper of empire, it is a thing rare and hard to keep, for both temper and distemper consist of contraries; but it is one thing to mingle contraries, another to interchange them. The answer of Apollonius to Vespasian is full of excellent instruction. Vespasian asked him, "What was Nero's overthrow?" He answered, "Nero could touch and tune the harp well; but in government sometimes he used to wind the pins too high, sometimes to let them down too low." And certain it is, that nothing destroyeth authority so much as the unequal and untimely interchange of power pressed too far, and relaxed too much.

This is true, that the wisdom of all these latter times in princes' affairs is rather fine deliveries, and shiftings of dangers and mischiefs, when they are near, than solid and grounded courses to keep them aloof; but this is but to try masteries with fortune, and let men beware how they neglect and suffer matter of trouble to be prepared. For no man can forbid the spark, nor tell whence it may come. The difficulties in princes' business are many and great; but the greatest difficulty is often in their own mind. For it is common with princes (saith Tacitus) to will contradictories: "Sunt plerumque regum voluntates vehementes, et inter se contrariæ;" for it is the solecism of power to think to command the end, and yet not to endure the mean.

Kings have to deal with their neighbors, their wives, their children, their prelates or clergy, their nobles, their second nobles or gentlemen, their merchants, their commons, and their men of war; and from all these arise dangers, if care and circumspection be not used.

First, for their neighbors, there can no general rule be given (the occasions are so variable), save one which ever holdeth; which is, that princes do keep due sentinel, that none of their neighbors do overgrow so (by increase of territory, by embracing of trade, by approaches, or the like), as they become more able to annoy them than they were; and this is generally the work of standing counsels to foresee and to hinder it. During that triumvirate of kings, King Henry the Eighth of England, Francis the First, King of France, and Charles the Fifth, Emperor, there was such a watch kept that none of the three could win a palm of ground, but the other two would straightways balance it, either by confederation, or, if need were, by a war; and would not, in any wise, take up peace at interest; and the like was done by that league (which Guicciardini saith was the security of Italy) made between Ferdinando, King of Naples, Lorenzius Medicis, and Ludovicus Sforza, potentates, the one of Florence, the other of Milan. Neither is the opinion of some of the schoolmen to be received, that a war cannot justly be made, but upon a precedent injury or provocation; for there is no question, but a just fear of an imminent danger, though there be no blow given, is a lawful cause of a war.

For their wives, there are cruel examples of them. Livia is infamed for the poisoning of her husband; Roxolana, Solyman's wife, was the destruction of that renowned prince, Sultan Mustapha, and otherwise troubled his house and succession; Edward the Second of England's Queen had the principal hand in the deposing and murder of her husband.

This kind of danger is then to be feared chiefly when the wives have plots for the raising of their own children, or else that they be advoutresses.

For their children, the tragedies likewise of dangers from them have been many; and generally the entering of fathers into suspicion of their children hath been ever unfortunate. The destruction of Mustapha (that we named before) was so fatal to Solyman's line, as the succession of the Turks from Solyman until this day is suspected to be untrue, and of strange blood; for that Selymus the Second was thought to be supposititious. The destruction of Crispus, a young prince of rare towardness, by Constantinus the Great, his father, was in like manner fatal to his house; for both Constantinus and Constance, his sons, died violent deaths; and Constantius, his other son, did little better, who died indeed of sickness, but after that Julianus had taken arms against him. The destruction of Demetrius, son to Philip the Second of Macedon, turned upon the father, who died of repentance. And many like examples there are; but few or none where the fathers had good by such distrust, except it were where the sons were up in open arms against them; as was Selymus the First against Bajazet, and the three sons of Henry the Second, King of England.

For their prelates, when they are proud and great, there is also danger from them; as it was in the times of Anselmus and Thomas Becket, Archbishops of Canterbury, who, with their crosiers, did almost try it with the king's sword; and yet they had to deal with stout and haughty kings; William Rufus, Henry the First, and Henry the Second. The danger is not from that state, but where it hath a dependence of foreign authority; or where the churchmen come in and are elected, not by the collation of the King, or particular patrons, but by the people.

For their nobles, to keep them at a distance it is not amiss; but to depress them may make a king more absolute, but less safe, and less able to perform anything that he desires. I have noted it in my History of King Henry the Seventh of England, who depressed his nobility, whereupon it came to pass that his times were full of difficulties and troubles; for the nobility, though they continued loyal unto him, yet did they not coöperate with him in his business; so that, in effect, he was fain to do all things himself.

For their second nobles, there is not much danger from them, being a body dispersed. They may sometimes discourse high, but that doth little hurt; besides, they are a counterpoise to the higher nobility, that they